BALLOON ANIMALS

• • • • • • • • • •

Barb Whiter

Published 2003 by Mud Puddle Books, Inc., 54 W. 21st St., Suite 601, New York, NY 10010, USA
Originally Published 2001, Hinkler Books Pty Ltd., 17-23 Redwood Drive, Dingley, Victoria, 3172, Australia
Copyright © 2001 by Redwood Publishing Group. All rights reserved.
Without limiting the rights under copyright above, no part of this publication may be reproduced, stored in or introduced into a retrieval system, or transmitted in any form or by any means (electronic, mechanical, photocopying, recording, or otherwise), without prior written permission of Hinkler Books Pty Ltd.
ISBN: 1-59412-023-4 • Made in China.

MUD PUDDLE BOOKS, INC.
New York, New York

Contents

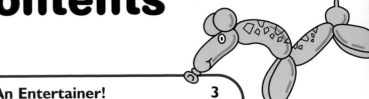

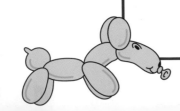

Becoming a Balloon Entertainer!

While there's absolutely nothing wrong with just wanting to create these fabulous, brightly colored Balloon Animals for yourself alone, we're betting once you've created your first real Balloon Animal you'll want to show off your skills to your family, friends and even friendly strangers!

In other words – you'll be a balloon entertainer!

It's a great way to be invited to parties, but really, it's also lots of fun – for you and your audiences. You could be asked to entertain at your school's fundraising fete, church garage sale or even take yourself along to a weekend market and become a roving balloon entertainer – the sky's the limit!

This skill is also known as Balloon Sculpture and the balloons you're using are called modeling balloons. It's probably only useful to know the term when you've used up all the balloons with this activity pack and you need to find out where to buy more. If you say you want to buy the long, thin, sausage-shaped balloons, the retailer will know what you want anyway!

As with any new skill, perfection doesn't come overnight and, although getting a good result quickly is possible with Balloon Sculpture, your skills will increase with practice.

If you want to move into entertaining with Balloon Animals, here are a few tips:

✔ Blow up the balloons you are going to need for your performance before you arrive. Watching someone blow up a balloon is not entertaining!

✔ Learn some 'patter' or some stories. Watching you create a Balloon Animal can be fun for one or two, but not for a whole performance. There needs to be something else for the audience to focus on, and that's where your stories or jokes will come in handy.

✔ Get used to giving away your pride-and-joys – however good they look! Remember you have the skill and can make another – even better – one!

✔ For performances, keep a black felt-tip pen in a handy pocket for drawing on mouths and eyes for your animals – it gives a real personal touch.

✔ If a balloon does burst during a performance, collect all the bits and put them somewhere safe away from young children and babies – they can be dangerous if they try to eat them! (This advice goes for practicing at home too, if you have younger brothers or sisters.)

✔ Finally, and always, HAVE FUN with your talent!

Getting Started
Inflating balloons, tying knots and safety

You'll spend lots of time inflating balloons and tying knots when creating Balloon Animals. They are things which need to be done carefully.

It is not cool to burst balloons for fun. The sound scares cats and dogs, not to mention your mom and your younger brothers and sisters, and as for babies, well, it's just something they don't need to hear! So don't do it! Anyway, it's a waste of a great resource… do you think these things grow on trees?

If you burst a balloon by mistake, and you probably will, bend down and clean up the bits of balloon and throw them away before you start blowing up another balloon. The reason – balloon bits are a danger to any baby brothers or sisters who may crawl about, find them and put them in their mouths, as well as to pets who may do the same – they could choke.

Don't try to blow up these modeling balloons using your lungs – it's too hard – that's why we've provided the balloon pump with this kit! Easy! Remember to hang on to the end of the balloon while it's over the nozzle of the pump and you're pumping air in. The instructions for each animal will tell you how long to make the balloon when you're pumping it up. When you take the inflated balloon off the pump, you'll need to tie a knot in the end just like with any other balloon.

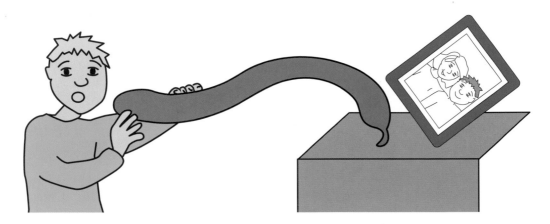

So, you're ready to blow up your first balloon. A little tip is to 'soften' the balloon first. Do this by keeping the balloons warm (but not in front of a heater or a fire!) – just a gentle rub between your hands and a few gentle stretches on the first part of the balloon before you blow it up will do the trick.

Blow up these balloons in an empty space. When they are uninflated they are only about 30 cm (1 foot) long and really skinny. Once air is in them, they can be over a meter (about 3 feet) long and waving about all over the place with a 5 cm (2 inch) diameter; mom's vases and special ornaments could be the victims if you blow up balloons too close.

It's important to put just enough air in each balloon. Even when the instructions say to fully inflate the balloon, just let a little bit of air out before you tie it. It makes it easier to tie the balloon knot if you squeeze the air towards the other end as you tie.

Finally, for all the reasons we've already mentioned, don't ever put a balloon in your mouth and keep them away from your eyes and other people's eyes. If you stick to these commonsense precautions, you and your friends can have hours of fun and enjoyment being balloon sculptors!

Basic twists...let's lock it in

The best way to learn the basic twists is to start now! So, inflate a balloon to about 45 cm (17.5 inches) long and tie it off. The twist you'll use most is the Lock Twist, so here's how to do it.

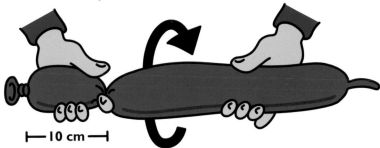

├──10 cm──┤

1. Hold the balloon gently. With your left hand at the knot end you need to measure down 10 cm (4 inches) and gently squeeze the balloon together with your thumb and first finger (see illustration). Yes, right down, so you can feel your other finger on the other side of the balloon!

2. Keep holding this tight, while at the same time, with your other hand, make two full turns of the balloon (see illustration). Don't let go!

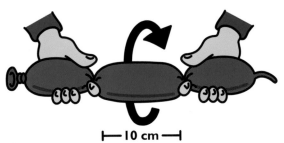

├──10 cm──┤

3. Move your right hand down the balloon another 10 cm (4 inches) – while your left hand continues to hold on to the twist you've just done – and again gently squeeze the balloon together with your thumb and first finger. Now twist the rest of the balloon with the right hand – making two full turns.

4. You can let go with your squeezing thumb and first fingers now but keep hold of the twisted balloon. Get ready for a tricky bit now.

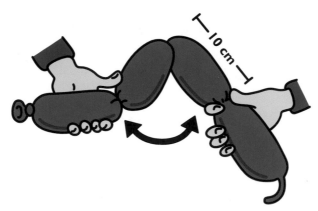

5. Fold the balloon over at the second twist so you are able to hold it with your left hand's thumb and first finger (see illustration) – so you are holding both twists in the one hand.

6. Move your right hand down yet another 10 cm (4 inches) along the balloon, squeeze in another 10 cm (4 inch) bubble and twist two full turns (see illustration).

7. Hold the first twist and the last twist together between your thumb and first finger and twist the two middle bubbles two full turns (see illustration).

8. Hey presto! This now locks your balloon twists together and you can let go! Can you see the two ears and a nose of some animal appearing? Well done! If you're not happy, go back and try again – and again – because you need to get this Lock Twist right before you can make any animals.

Loop Twist

An easy variation of the Basic Twist to help create great ears or legs for an animal.

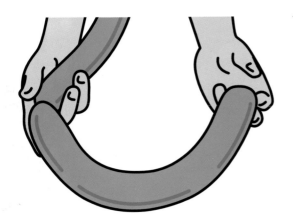 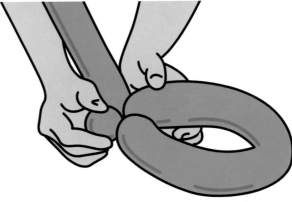

1. Inflate a balloon to the required length. For practice, inflate to 45 cm (17.5 inches) again. Make a twist at either end of the balloon – remember a twist is just two full turns of the balloon made while it's being squeezed together gently by your thumb and first finger (see illustration).

2. Now simply wrap one end of the balloon around the other to lock the twists together (see illustration).

There are other twists used in making Balloon Animals, but these are the basic twists you'll need to know for your first few animals.

Decorate your balloon

Many people think Balloon Animals come alive with just the addition of a couple of eyes and maybe some body markings.

This can be easily achieved by using a black permanent marker – just on the balloon, of course!

So let's start making Balloon Animals!

Now Let's Have Some Fun

Your first animal - Is It a Dog?

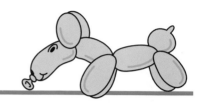

So, you've made two ears and a nose in the practice for the Basic Twists – easy, right? Well, let's make a whole animal this time – it'll probably end up looking like a dog – or any animal with four legs!

1. Inflate your balloon to create a bubble about 45 cm (17.5 inches) long.

2. Twist a 6 cm (2.25 inch) bubble for a nose, and twist two more bubbles about 5-6 cm (2 - 2.25 inches) long to create the ears. Remember to hold on to these bubbles because you've now got to lock them in place (see illustration).

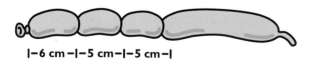

|–6 cm –|–5 cm –|–5 cm –|

3. You remember? Just fold over bubbles two and three and Lock Twist them into place. You've now repeated everything you learned when doing the practice of Basic Twists (see illustration).

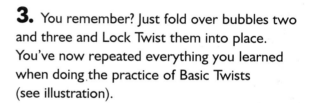

4. Continue by gripping and twisting another 5 cm (2 inch) bubble down from the ears to make the neck.

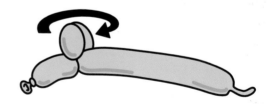

5. Hold this bubble and twist two more bubbles about 6 cm (.25 inches) long to create the front legs (see illustration).

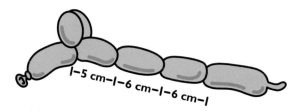

6. Fold over the legs and Lock Twist them into place together. Don't you love the sound of those squeaks!

7. Create the body by twisting a 6 cm (2.25 inch) bubble from the legs and add two more 6 cm (2.25 inch) bubbles to create the back legs (see illustration).

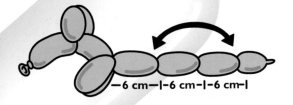

8. Fold over the legs again and Lock Twist them together (see illustration).

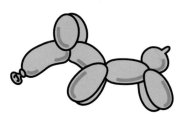

9. Twist everything straight and you have a 3 cm (1.25 inch) bubble left for the tail! Congratulations! Your first animal is ready for a personality – just draw on a face with a felt-tip pen – eyes and a mouth usually work (see illustration).

Poodle

You've all seen a poodle. It's a dog whose coat is cut in different ways to an average pet dog – so balloon sculptors have to create a different head and tail. Easy, just follow the instructions carefully.

1. Your balloon needs to be inflated to around 80 cm (2 ft 7 ins) for this special dog.

2. To get the right look straight away, twist a 15 cm (6 inch) bubble for the nose. Yes, it's much longer than usual! (Don't let it go.)

3. Twist another 20 cm (8 inch) bubble which will become the specially-shaped head.

4. This is a bit tricky so read the instructions carefully and bend this bubble into a ring shape and Lock Twist it (see illustration).

5. Bend the long nose bubble backwards into the ring and push it about half through (see illustration). Just a tip, it's probably easier to try to roll the head over the other bubble.

6. Twist a tiny 2 cm (0.75 inch) neck bubble, and two 10 cm (4 inch) bubbles for the front legs (see illustration).

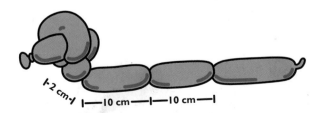

7. Lock Twist the front legs together (see illustration).

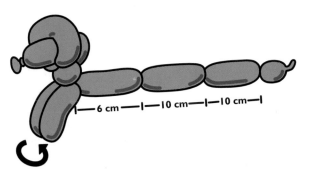

8. Twist a 6 cm (2.25 inch) bubble for the body and two more 10 cm (4 inch) bubbles to make the back legs.

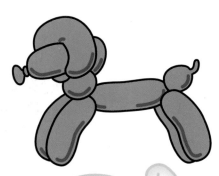

9. Lock Twist the back legs together (see illustration).

10. Straighten all the bubbles so your dog looks nearly complete. There's just a 5 cm (2 inch) bubble left with a bit of uninflated balloon.

11. Hold the uninflated part of the balloon in one hand and gently squeeze the tail bubble at the same time (see illustration). A tiny bobble will appear right on the end of the balloon. A perfect poodle tail!

Swan

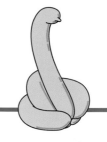

Here's a simple version made with one white balloon, but we've also included instructions to make a larger swan with two balloons. Make a family!

1. Fully inflate your white balloon, leaving just a short tail end uninflated.

2. Create two bubbles, each about 35 cm (1ft) long (see illustration).

3. Loop both these bubbles and twist the ends together. You have two large loops and a straight portion of balloon left (see illustration).

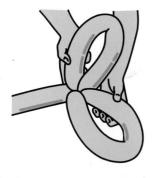

4. Tuck one loop inside the other, arranging the loops carefully to create the swan's body with the wings sticking up (see illustration).

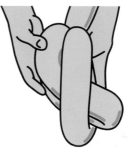

5. Create the elegant curved neck of the swan by pinching the end of the balloon and pulling it around down to the 'chest' of the swan. This will give a beautiful curve.

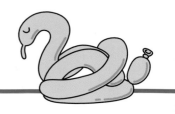

Now these swans are really beautiful as they are, but if you want to show off your new talents, you can create a larger swan using two balloons. Read on:

1. Inflate a white balloon fully.

2. Tie in a loop (see illustration).

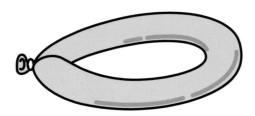

3. Now carefully twist the loop into a figure of eight, leaving the knot at the end (see illustration).

4. Bend the loops so they curve, and then tuck the knotted loop into the other one (see illustration).

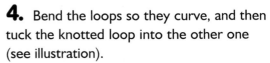

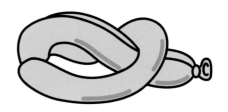

5. Inflate another balloon (white, of course) with a 90 cm (3 ft) bubble.

6. Twist a 15 cm (6 inch) bubble for the tail and Lock Twist it to the knot in the first balloon.

7. Twist a 20 cm (8 inch) bubble for the body and Lock Twist it to the middle of the figure of eight

8. Hold the uninflated end of the balloon tightly between your thumb and first finger and roll the balloon in your hand. This will have the effect of curving the neck. Persevere, because the more you curve the neck the better the swan will look (see illustration).

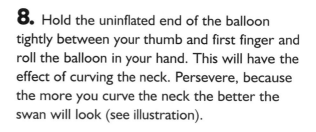

9. Straighten the sculpture out and draw eyes (see illustration).

Giraffe

Making this giraffe will show you how easy it is to make different animals. A yellow or orange balloon is good for this one.

1. Inflate your balloon to around 75 cm (2 ft 5 inches).

2. Twist an 8 cm (3.25 inch) bubble to form the giraffe's head, then twist two 3 cm (1.25 inch) bubbles to form small ears – cute eh?

3. Lock Twist the ears (see illustration).

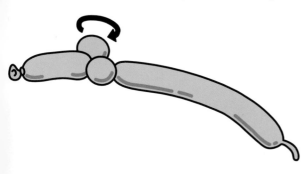

4. Twist a really long bubble for the giraffe's long neck – about 20 cm (8 inches) should be right. Then twist two 10 cm (4 inch) bubbles for the two front legs.

5. Lock Twist the front legs together (see illustration).

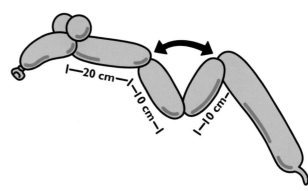

6. You only need a 5 cm (2 inch) bubble for the giraffe's body, so twist that and two 9 cm (3.5 inch) bubbles for the back legs. (Look at a picture of a giraffe and you'll see its back legs are slightly shorter than its front ones.)

7. Lock Twist the back legs together (see illustration)

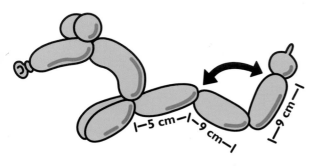

8. Make sure the tail bubble looks right and then draw a face and some body markings on your new giraffe.

Horse

A horse could also be a dog…but slightly different! Think of all the variations you could make. You'll end up with a herd.

1. Inflate a balloon to about 75 cm (2 ft 5 inches) long. Tie the knot tight enough to make sure the air doesn't get out, but not as tight as you usually do.

2. Twist a bubble 8 cm (3.25 inches) long for the head.

3. Twist a bubble only 3 cm (1.25 inches) long for the first ear. This new look for ears is called a Pinch Twist. Once you have your small bubble, bend it over into a tight ring and Lock Twist it to the head separately.

4. Twist another 3 cm (1.25 inch) bubble and treat it the same way by bending it into a tight ring, then Lock Twist it to the head. See, the ears now have a slight curve to them. (Or if this isn't working for you, just create a pair of ears the same way as we've done previously.)

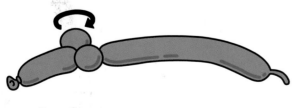

5. Grip the knot at the nose, and roll it slightly so it moves to the end of the balloon (see illustration).

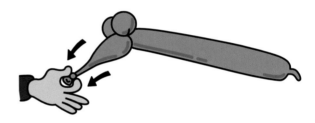

6. Squeeze the head bubble which will make the nose bulge out a bit at the end – just like a horse, right? (See illustration.)

7. Back to twisting. Make a 10 cm (4 inch) twist for the neck and two more 10 cm (4 inch) twists for the front legs.

8. Bend the two bubbles over and Lock Twist the front legs together.

9. Adjust the neck bubble if necessary to make the head lean forward.

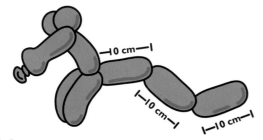

10. Twist a 10 cm (4 inch) body bubble and two more 10 cm (4 inch) bubbles for the back legs.

11. Lock Twist the back legs together (see illustration).

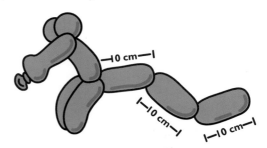

12. To create the tail from the 5 cm (2 inch) bubble and extra balloon you have left, gently squeeze the tail bubble until the air fills all of the extra balloon and then bend it down slightly.

13. Personalize your horse by drawing on a face, with a hairy forehead, a mane and a tail.

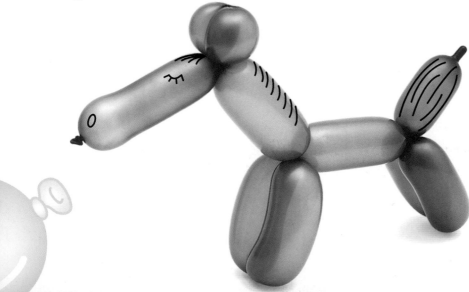

Mouse

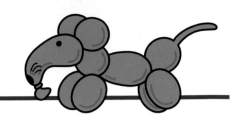

This is harder to make because mice are so small! You need to make your bubbles as small as you can, but beware, if you make them too small, they just disappear before you can Lock Twist them! A hint is to push some of the air out of the bubbles before you begin to twist.

1. Inflate the balloon so it is only 20 cm (8 inches) long.

2. Twist a bubble 5 cm (2 inches) long for the head. This is the biggest bubble you will create for the mouse.

3. Twist a 3 cm (1.25 inch) bubble for the ear, and bend it over and twist it to the head.

4. Similarly, twist another 3 cm (1.25 inch) bubble, bend it over and twist it to the head for the second ear (see illustration).

5. Pull on the knot hard to bring the head down so it looks more like a mouse (see illustration).

6. Now for a series of really small bubbles. First twist a 2 cm (0.75 inch) neck bubble and two 2 cm (0.75 inch) bubbles for the front legs.

7. Lock Twist the front legs together (see illustration).

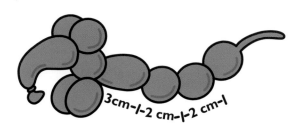

8. Twist a 3 cm (1.25 inch) body bubble, and then two more 2 cm (0.75 inch) bubbles for the back legs.

9. Lock Twist the back legs together (see illustration).

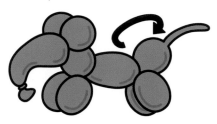

10. Now there should be a 2 cm (0.75 inch) tail bubble left and a really long tail (uninflated balloon).

11. Draw a face on your mouse, including whiskers, of course.

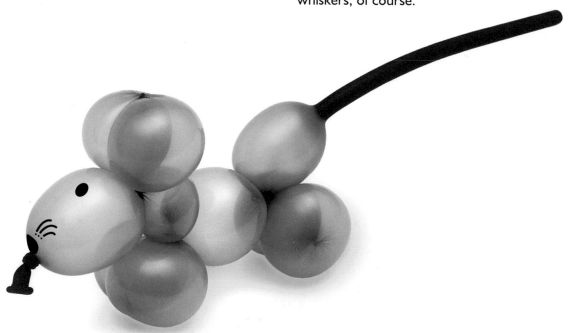

Elephant

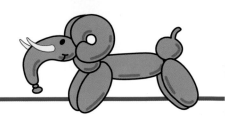

Have you heard that the only thing an elephant fears is a mouse? Well, you've created the mouse, now let's see you create the elephant.

1. Inflate your balloon to 90 cm (3 ft).

2. Twist a long 20 cm (8 inch) bubble which will be the trunk and head of the elephant.

3. Twist a 20 cm (8 inch) bubble for the ear.

4. Bend the ear bubble over and Lock Twist it to the head (see illustration).

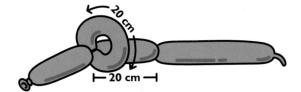

5. Twist another 20 cm (8 inch) bubble for the other ear, bend it over and Lock Twist it to the head (see illustration).

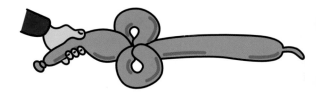

6. Now hold the trunk and squeeze hard so air travels up to the head. At the same time pull down on the trunk and it will look amazingly like an elephant's trunk hanging down (see illustration).

7. Twist a small 3 cm (1.25 inch) bubble to create the neck and twist two 5 cm (2 inch) bubbles to make front legs.

8. Lock Twist the front legs (see illustration).

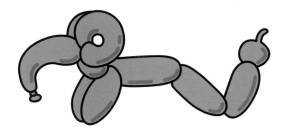

9. Twist a 5 cm (2 inch) bubble for the body, plus two 4 cm (1.5 inch) bubbles for the back legs (yes, just a little shorter than the front legs).

10. Lock Twist the back legs to the body (see illustration).

11. There will be about 3 cm (1.25 inches) left over as a tail bubble.

12. Draw on a face – small eyes and two tusks are essential.

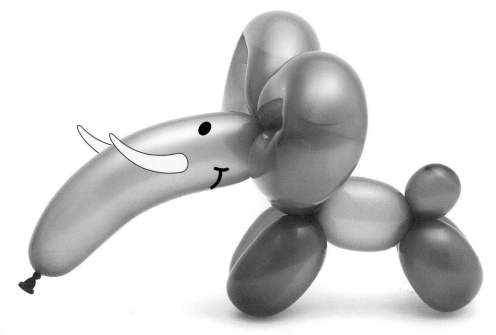

Octopus

This is actually quite easy to make, although it looks hard because there are so many balloons and quite a few steps to follow. It looks spectacular when it's finished because of the colors and shape of the octopus. Great for summer fun!

1. Fully inflate three balloons (all different colors for fun!) but just before you tie them off, let out a little air from each to soften them.

2. Lay the balloons side by side and then Lock Twist them together in the middle (see illustration).

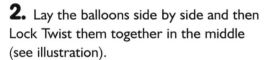

3. Make sure the twist is at the top.

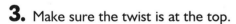

4. Measure down about 25 cm (10 inches) and Lock Twist them together again (see illustration).

5. Inflate another balloon leaving a 5 cm (2 inch) tail uninflated.

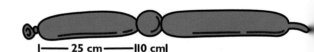

I—5 cm—I

6. Twist a 25 cm (10 inch) bubble and then a 10 cm (4 inch) bubble, this will be one eye.

I—— 25 cm ——I10 cmI

7. Bend the eye bubble over and Lock Twist into place.

8. Twist a 5 cm (2 inch) bubble and then another 10 cm (4 inch) bubble for the second eye. Bend over and Lock Twist.

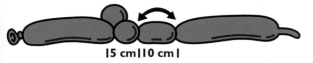

|5 cm|10 cm|

9. Insert this balloon with the eyes behind one of the head pieces of the already-created monster (see illustration), and ensure the eyes are in the right place.

10. Pull these last two legs down and Lock Twist into place with the others.

11. Draw eyes on the eye bubbles with a felt-tip pen (see illustration).

Rhinoceros

Let's see how easy it is to make a rhinoceros. The elephant and the rhinoceros can keep each other company.

1. Inflate the balloon to 80 cm (2 ft 7 inches) long.

2. This time we'll begin at the tail, so twist a 2 cm (0.75 inch) tail bubble and two 5 cm (2 inch) bubbles to create the back legs.

3. Fold over the legs and Lock Twist to the tail. (see illustration).

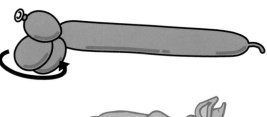

4. Now twist a 5 cm (2 inch) bubble for the rhino's body and another two 5 cm (2 inch) bubbles for the front legs. Fold these legs over and Lock Twist to the body.

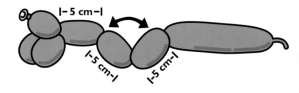

5. Don't panic if it looks as if there is far too much balloon left for the rest of the rhino – we'll use it!

6. Next twist a tiny 2 cm (0.75 inch) bubble for the neck and twist a 3 cm (1.25 inch) bubble to create one ear. Bend the ear over and Lock Twist it to the neck (see illustration).

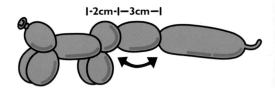

7. Twist another 3 cm (1.25 inch) ear bubble, fold it over and Lock Twist it with the other. There should be about 10 cm (4 inches) of inflated bubble left, plus some balloon.

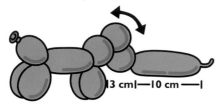

3 cm—10 cm—

8. Pinch the balloon really tightly at the end of the head bubble and bend the head upwards (see illustration). This will stretch the balloon under the chin and tip the rhino's horn up.

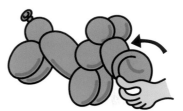

9. Draw in a face. The eye should be small and halfway along the head (see illustration).

Wasp, Bee, Dragonfly or a Bird?

This is a really easy one. Using the one balloon you can change your mind halfway through to make a different animal. As they're so easy, why not make two or three, or one of each?

1. Inflate your balloon until it is 80 cm (2 ft 7 inches) long.

2. At the knot end twist a 5 cm (2 inch) bubble and at the tail end twist a 6 cm (2.25 inch) bubble.

3. Bend over these bubbles and Lock Twist them together. You now have a large loop (see illustration).

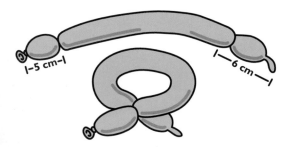

|—5 cm—| |—6 cm—|

4. Halfway around this loop, nip the balloon between your thumb and first finger and Lock Twist it to the neck.

NIP!

5. This is the point where you decide what you are creating. If you draw a face at the knot end and some stripes it will mean you'll have a wasp or a bee. If you choose to create a bird, you'll draw a face at the 'pointed' end so the uninflated end becomes a beak. If you decide on a dragonfly, you draw the face at the knot end, but squeeze air into the tail bubble to fill the point.

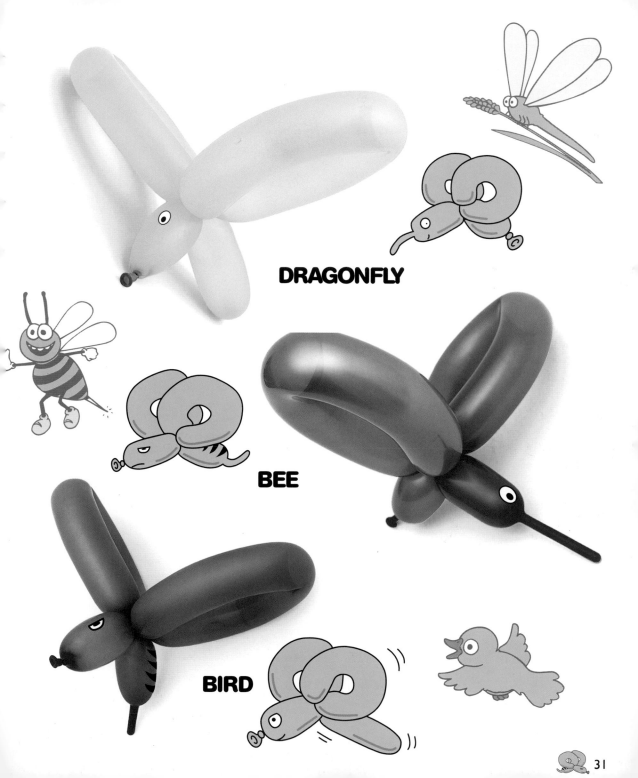

DRAGONFLY

BEE

BIRD

31

Crocodile

Use a green balloon, of course, and then you can have one or more crocodiles in your bath tonight!

1. You'll need a balloon inflated to 85 cm (2 ft 9 inches) long.

2. Twist a 10 cm (4 inch) bubble to create the head, and a 5 cm (2 inch) bubble to create an eye.

3. Bend the eye bubble over and Lock Twist it to the head. Twist another 5 cm (2 inch) eye bubble and bend this one over Lock Twist it to the head too, next to the first eye. (see illustration).

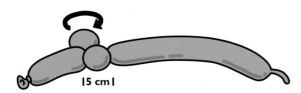

4. Just a tiny 3 cm (1.25 inch) bubble is needed for the neck and a 15 cm (6 inch) bubble for the first front leg. Bend this leg over and Lock Twist it to the neck.

5. Twist a second 15 cm (6 inch) bubble for the second front leg, bend it over and Lock Twist it to the neck too (see illustration).

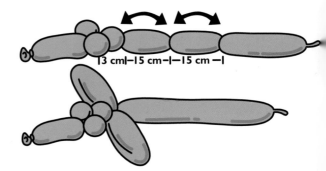

6. Twist a 10 cm (4 inch) bubble for the body, plus a 15 cm (6 inch) bubble for the first back leg. Bend the leg over and Lock Twist into place.

7. Twist another 15 cm (6 inch) back leg, bend it over and Lock Twist it to the body too (see illustration).

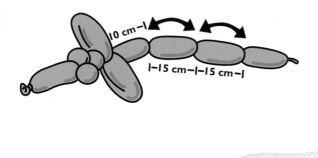

8. There is a 10 cm (4 inch) bubble left. Squeeze the air to fill the whole tail.

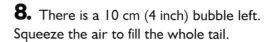

9. Make sure the legs are straight and then draw on a suitable face, not forgetting the markings on the back of the croc!

Baby Dinosaur

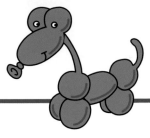

You'll need to use your imagination with this one - especially when you decorate it at the end. It's fun to finish but demanding to make, so pay attention! When twisting all these small bubbles it's a good trick to remember to squeeze some air out as you twist.

1. Inflate your balloon to 20 cm (8 inches).

2. Twist a small 2 cm (0.75 inch) bubble to create a small nose – well, we did say it was a baby dinosaur!

3. Twist another 2 cm (0.75 inch) bubble, this time for an ear. Bend the ear over and Lock Twist it to the nose.

4. Don't forget to squeeze as you twist – and twist another 2 cm (0.75 inch) ear bubble, bend it over and Lock Twist it (see illustration).

5. Now this move is tricky and one we've not done before. Squeeze all the air out of the neck for 5 cm (2 inches). Push the air along the balloon but not right to the end (see illustration).

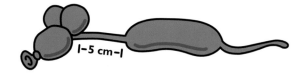

6. Twist a small 2 cm (0.75 inch) bubble at the end of this skinny neck.

7. Then twist a 3 cm (1.25 inch) bubble for a front leg. Fold it over and Lock Twist it in place.

8. Squeeze twist another 3 cm (1.25 inch front leg, fold it over and lock twist it (see illustration).

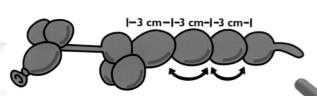

|—3 cm—|—3 cm—|—3 cm—|

9. Not forgetting to squeeze as you twist, make a 3 cm (1.25 inch) bubble for the body, and a 3 cm (1.25 inch) bubble for one back leg.

10. Fold the back leg bubble over the body bubble and Lock Twist in place.

11. Twist anonther 3 cm (1.25 inch) bubble for the other back leg, fold it over and Lock Twist into place. There is a little tail left to jauntily stick up (see illustration).

12. Paint on a face with your felt-tip pen— maybe some little fangs and eyes.

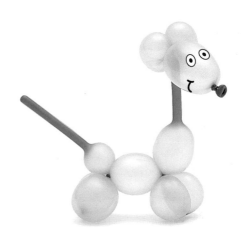

Big Fish

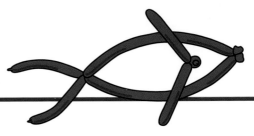

You'll always have company if you keep this fish in your bedroom or bathroom. He's big enough to have a personality of his own. Try using different colored balloons to obtain different effects – bright colors will give you tropical fish, while paler greys and blues will give you cool water fish.

1. Nearly fully inflate two balloons, leaving a tiny bit uninflated at the end.

2. At the knot end of each balloon twist a 4 cm (1.5 inch) bubble and then interlock them by twisting the balloons together. These bubbles form your fish's mouth (see illustration).

3. Inflate another balloon (in another color) to measure about 85 cm (2 ft 9 inches), leaving a short uninflated end.

4. Make two long bubbles about 20 cm (8 inches) long each and twist the ends together (see illustration).

5. Now make a small bubble, probably only 5 cm (2 inches) long, bend it back on itself and twist to the other bubbles to hold.

6. Create two long bubbles of equal length from the rest of the balloon and twist the ends together – now you have fins!

7. Slide the fins into the first two joined balloons – carefully because if they rub together too much they may burst (see illustration).

8. Grab the open ends of the first two balloons and interlock them to form the tail (see illustration).

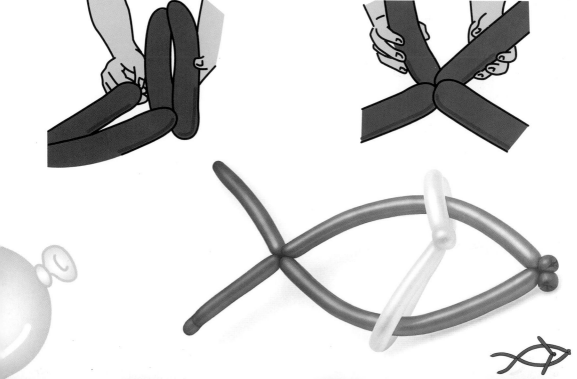

Caterpillar

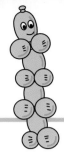

This is a caterpillar which can stand or crawl along the floor. Add eyes and little feet with a felt-tip pen and make more than one because they can all have different personalities. This sculpture is made with just the one twist – called a Pinch Twist – which has been used on other animals in the book to make cute ears. You'll soon see how it works.

Don't despair if you don't get this 'right' first time, as the secret is in achieving a balanced look with all the 'feet' the same size – and this is hard!

1. Inflate a balloon leaving a long 14 cm (5.5 inch) tail at the end. Now you've done the inflating, gently let out quite a bit of air to soften the balloon. You have to do this because of all the small bubbles needed to create your caterpillar – they use lots of air and if the balloon is too full it will burst! Trust me on this!

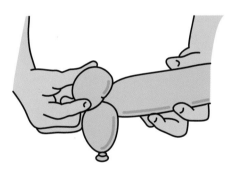

2. Twist a 4 cm (1.5 inch) bubble to be the head of the caterpillar, and then a 3 cm (1.25 inch) bubble. Hold both firmly.

3. Pinch and twist the second 3 cm (1.25 inch) bubble. You need to pinch both ends of this small bubble together and twist it twice. Do it gently and it bends back on itself. It is really hard, I know, but the end result is worth the effort. Keep practicing because it's the only 'locking' twist you do to create this cute caterpillar! (See illustration.)

4. Prepare another 3 cm (1.25 inch) bubble and Pinch Twist this one to match the other bubble. It now looks as if your caterpillar is gaining some feet (see illustration).

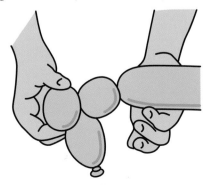

5. Once you have created the head and the first set of feet you continue in the same way until you reach the end of the balloon. So, make another two 3 cm (1.25 inch) bubbles, Pinch Twisting the second one to create the first side of 'feet'.

6. Make another 3 cm (1.25 inch) bubble and Pinch Twist it to match the previous one (see illustration), so after each second Pinch Twist you create a set of feet.

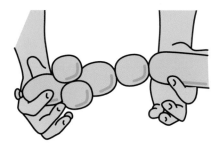

7. Continue to make another two 3 cm (1.25 inch) bubbles, Pinch twisting the second one to create the first side of 'feet'.

8. Make another 3 cm (1.25 inch) bubble and Pinch Twist it to match the previous one (see illustration).

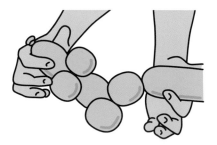

9. Make another two 3 cm (1.25 inch) bubbles, pinch twisting the second one to create the first side of 'feet'.

10. Make another 3 cm (1.25 inch) bubble and Pinch Twist it to match the previous one (see illustration).

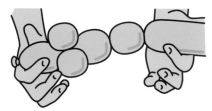

11. This should mean you are at the end of the balloon and your caterpillar has four sets of feet to stand up or crawl on (see illustration). Longer balloons can of course give longer caterpillars, but don't forget all the little bubbles take up a lot of air in the making, so leave lots of uninflated balloon when beginning.

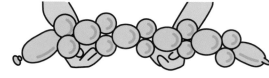

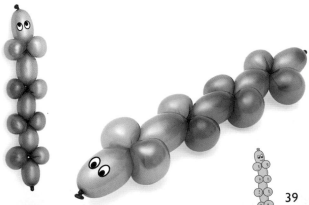

Teddy Bear

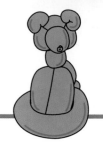

This is a cuddly teddy bear. It will sit by itself quite happily, but can also be transported about with you wherever you go – on your arm.

We think this animal and the next one, the cat, are harder to create than the other animals in this book. We hope you've enjoyed creating the easier animals and feel quite happy about tackling these new, harder animals. If you're not confident to do the teddy bear yet, why not go back and make more fish or dogs or another giraffe? Then, after you feel you've really got the hang of Balloon Sculpture, attempt the teddy bear. You can give it a go now!

1. You may need someone to help you hold the handful of twists you need to make the bear's face. Begin by inflating your balloon, leaving about a 12 cm (4.75 inch) uninflated end. Now it's inflated, gently release some of the air before you tie it off, making it softer.

2. Make a 5 cm (2 inch) bubble, then a 3 cm (1.25 inch) bubble, a 4 cm (1.5 inch) bubble, then three 3 cm (1.25 inch) bubbles and another 4 cm (1.5 inch) bubble – seven bubbles in all (see illustration). Got them in your hand? Good, don't let go!

3. Make the bear's face by twisting the two 4 cm (1.5 inch) bubbles together – this forms a circle of bubbles.

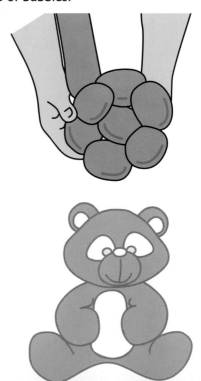

4. Push the first bubble (the one with the knot end) into the center of the circle so it sticks out the other side. Be careful here, as bubbles pushing and rubbing against each other could burst. You can see (in the illustration) the knot end becomes the teddy's nose.

5. Pinch Twist one of the 3 cm (1.25 inch) bubbles to make one ear. Now make the second ear on the opposite side with a 3 cm (1.25 inch) bubble (see illustration above). Now doesn't he look cute!

6. Create a 4 cm (1.5 inch) bubble for a neck, then twist two longer bubbles about 10 cm (4 inches) each for the front paws, then Lock Twist them together (see illustration).

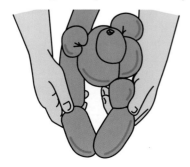

7. Now let's make him sit up for you. With the rest of the balloon make a small bubble at each end and Loop Twist them together (see illustration).

8. This creates a 'seat' for the bear and by pushing the front paws into the looped legs your bear will sit happily with you while you play or watch TV.

Cat

As we mentioned in Teddy Bear this is one of the harder animals.

We hope you've enjoyed creating the easier animals and feel quite happy about tackling these new, harder animals. If you're not confident to do the cat yet, why not go back and make more fish or dogs or another giraffe? Then, after you feel you've really got the hang of Balloon Sculpture, attempt the cat. Or…go for it now!

1. Inflate your balloon (perhaps yellow, orange or grey for a tabby cat) to create a 70 cm (2 ft 3 inch) bubble and tie off the balloon.

2. Squeeze and twist a 10 cm (4 inch) bubble for a nose, then a 6 cm (2.25 inch) bubble for one of the cat's cheeks.

3. This can be tricky. Keep holding the nose and cheek bubbles while at the same time twisting a 3 cm (1.25 inch) ear bubble (see illustration). Hang on!

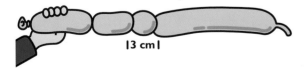

|3 cm|

4. Fold over the ear and Pinch Twist it to the cheek bubble (see illustration).

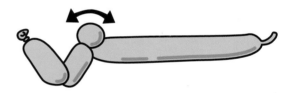

5. Twist another 3 cm (1.25 inch) bubble for the top of the cat's head.

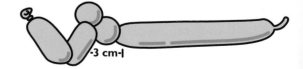

|-3 cm-|

6. Squeeze and twist another 3 cm (1.25 inch) bubble for the ear. Fold it over and Lock Twist it to the head bubble (see illustration).

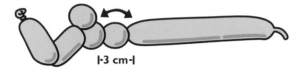

|-3 cm-|

7. Twist another 6 cm (2.25 inch) bubble to create the other cheek. Lock Twist it to the nose bubble (see illustration). You can see the head forming now.

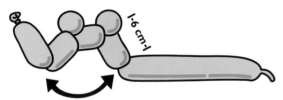

|-6 cm-|

8. Take the nose bubble and push it between the cheeks to rest about halfway through with the knot hidden at the back of the head (see illustration).

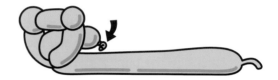

9. Well done! The head is probably the hardest part of the cat, so if you are happy with it, give yourself a pat on the back. Now let's continue with its body. Begin by twisting a 10 cm (4 inch) front leg.

Twirly Balloon Entertainer's Hat

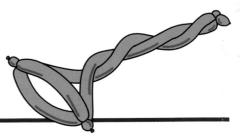

Once you can make three or four or more of these wonderful Balloon Animal Sculptures, you may like to put on a show for some friends. To give them some idea of what fun to look forward to, you could make this hat and wear it during the performance.

Or, just make it anyway and wear it to your next party – everyone will want to know how you did it!

1. Fully inflate two balloons, making sure they are the same length when inflated. Measure your head size now. For someone around 10 or 11 years old, 40 cm (1 ft 4 inches) would be around average, but don't worry if you are smaller or larger, just remember what your measurement is and divide it in half.

2. Make a small bubble in one balloon, and then twist this onto the second balloon at the measurement you came up with after measuring your head – it would be 20 cm (8 inches) in our example (see illustration).

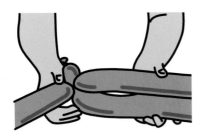

3. Now twist a small bubble in the second balloon and twist it onto the first balloon to complete the headband (see illustration). If you make lots of these hats you'll get to know the exact right length for you and then you can adjust it for younger kids or adults.

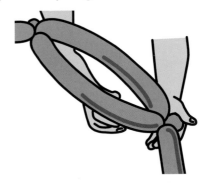

4. Now the real fun begins! While keeping the headband part steady, slowly curl the balloons around each other to make a spiral. Three or four turns are about right (see illustration).

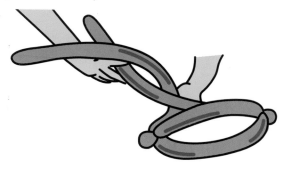

5. Right at the top of the spiral, pinch both balloons, twisting and locking them into position so they can't uncurl (see illustration). Now wear the hat with pride – and a great sense of fun!

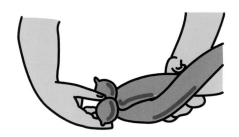

DOs and DON'Ts
Just a summary of what you have been doing!

Do keep your precious balloons in a sealed container in a cool, dark and dry place, well away from younger kids and pets.

Do cut your finger nails. If you've got this far, you've probably burst a few balloons. If you have long or uneven nails, you will burst even more!

Do use the pump provided to blow up the balloons.

Do stretch and warm the balloons gently before you blow them up.

Do practice and practice and practice – it becomes more fun when you are really, really good!

Do remember, homework comes before Balloon Sculpture practice!

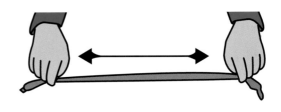

Don't use old and brittle balloons, they will burst. It's a certainty.

Don't put balloons in your mouth for any reason at all. No, not even to 'suck' a bubble at the end of the poodle's tail!

Don't burst balloons 'for fun' – it's not!

Don't work with your balloons in an enclosed area, near precious ornaments or near another person working with balloons. Tears will follow!

Don't leave burst balloon bits lying about – they're dangerous to small children and animals.

Oh, by the way, DO have lots of fun!